PLANET MARS

By Emily Kington

CONTENTS

First published in 2026 by Hungry Tomato Ltd
F15, Old Bakery Studios, Blewetts Wharf, Malpas Road,
Truro, Cornwall, TR1 1QH, UK.

A CIP catalog record for this book is available from the British Library.

ISBN 9781835696798

Manufactured in the USA

Discover more at
www.hungrytomato.com

Front cover image is an edited image of the Perseverance Rover.
Title page image is an edited image of Mars.
Contents page image is an edited image of Mars.

Words in **BOLD** can be found in the glossary.

WHERE IS MARS?

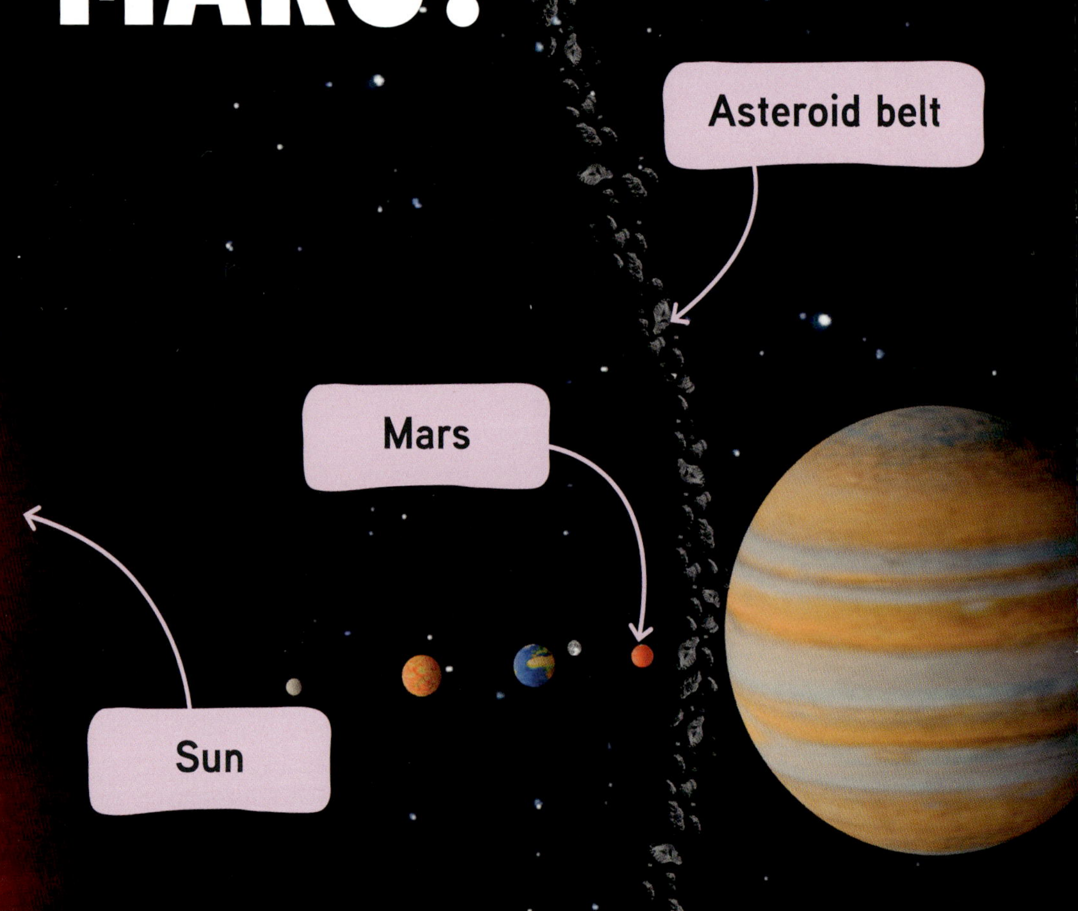

There are eight planets in our **solar system**. The planets travel around the Sun. Mars is the fourth planet from the Sun and lies between Earth and Jupiter.

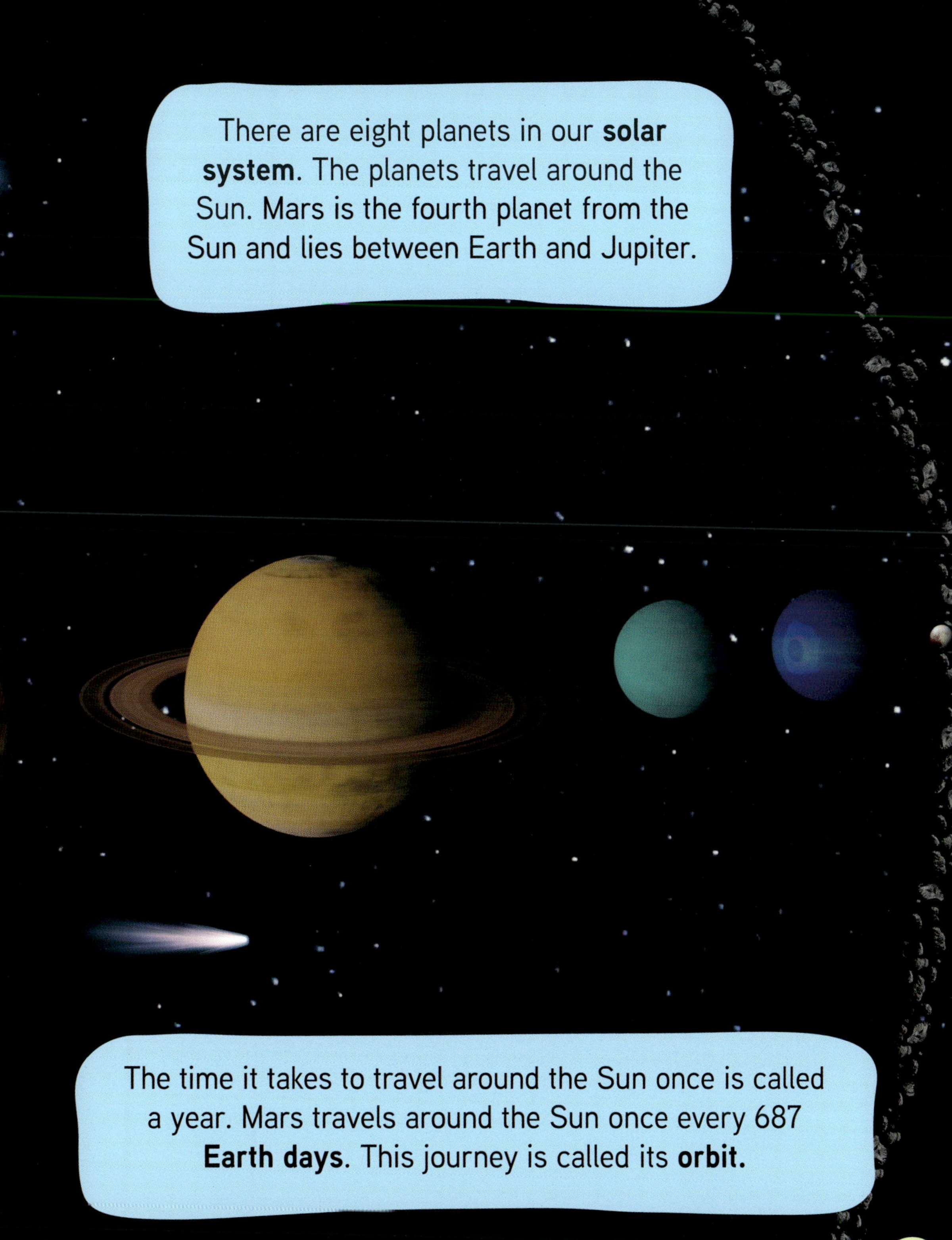

The time it takes to travel around the Sun once is called a year. Mars travels around the Sun once every 687 **Earth days**. This journey is called its **orbit.**

PLANET FACTS

Mars is often called the "Red Planet" because of its soil. The surface looks like a big, red, dusty desert!

Planets are always spinning. The time a planet takes to spin around once is called a day. A day on Mars is just 37 minutes longer than a day on Earth!

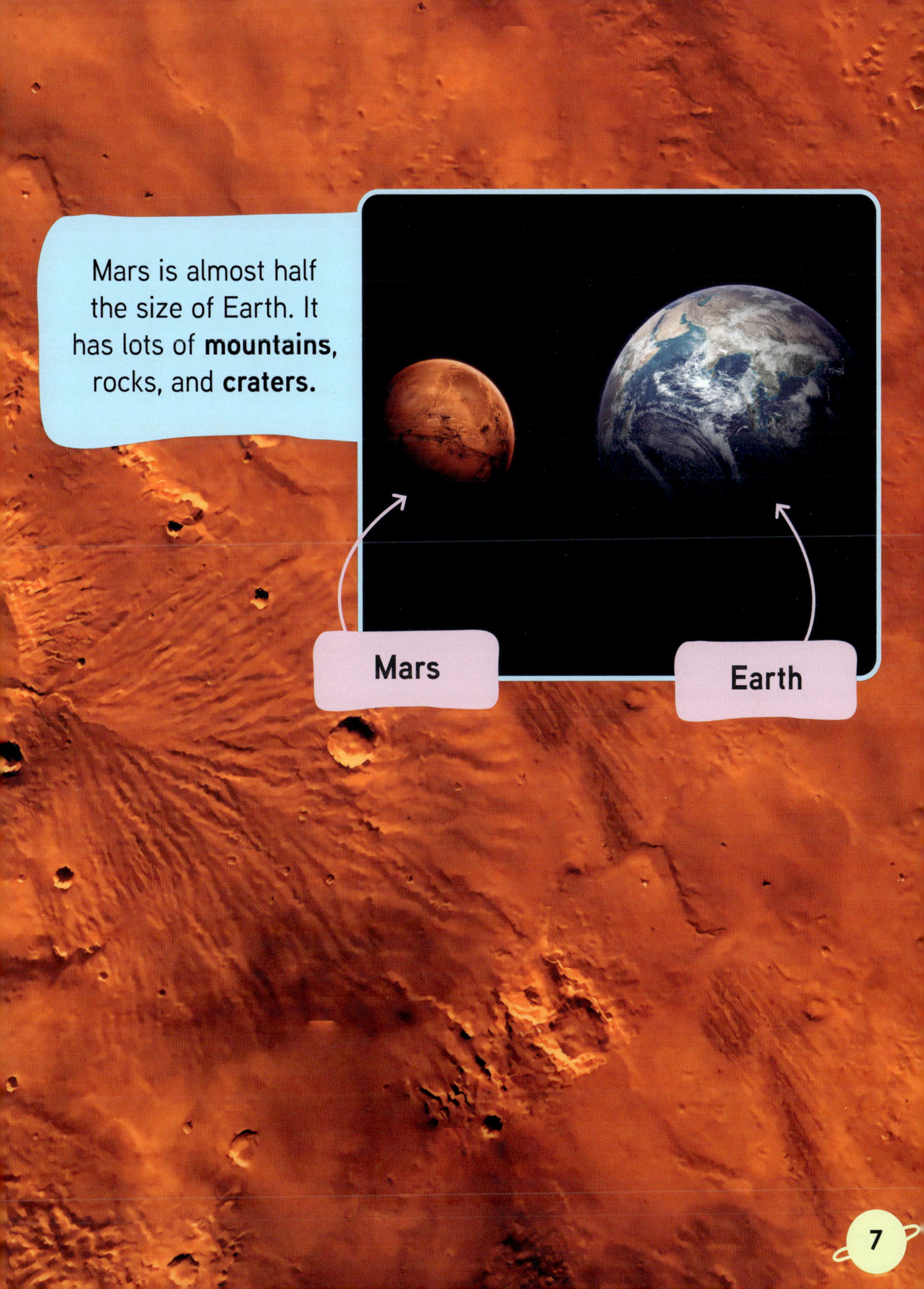
Mars is almost half the size of Earth. It has lots of **mountains,** rocks, and **craters.**
Mars
Earth

WHAT'S THE WEATHER LIKE?

Mars has a very thin **atmosphere,** mostly made of **carbon dioxide**. Heat easily escapes from it.

During the day the surface of Mars can reach 70 °F (20 °C), but at night it can get as cold as -225 °F (-153 °C)!

Mars is also very windy. It has huge dust storms that can last for weeks!

Mars has water ice under the surface of its north and south **poles** – just like Earth does!

MARS'S MOONS

Mars has two **moons** called Phobos and Deimos. They are both smaller than Earth's Moon.

These moons attract a lot of attention from scientists, who are planning missions to explore them in the future!

Scientists think they might both have been captured **asteroids** that came from the **asteroid belt.**

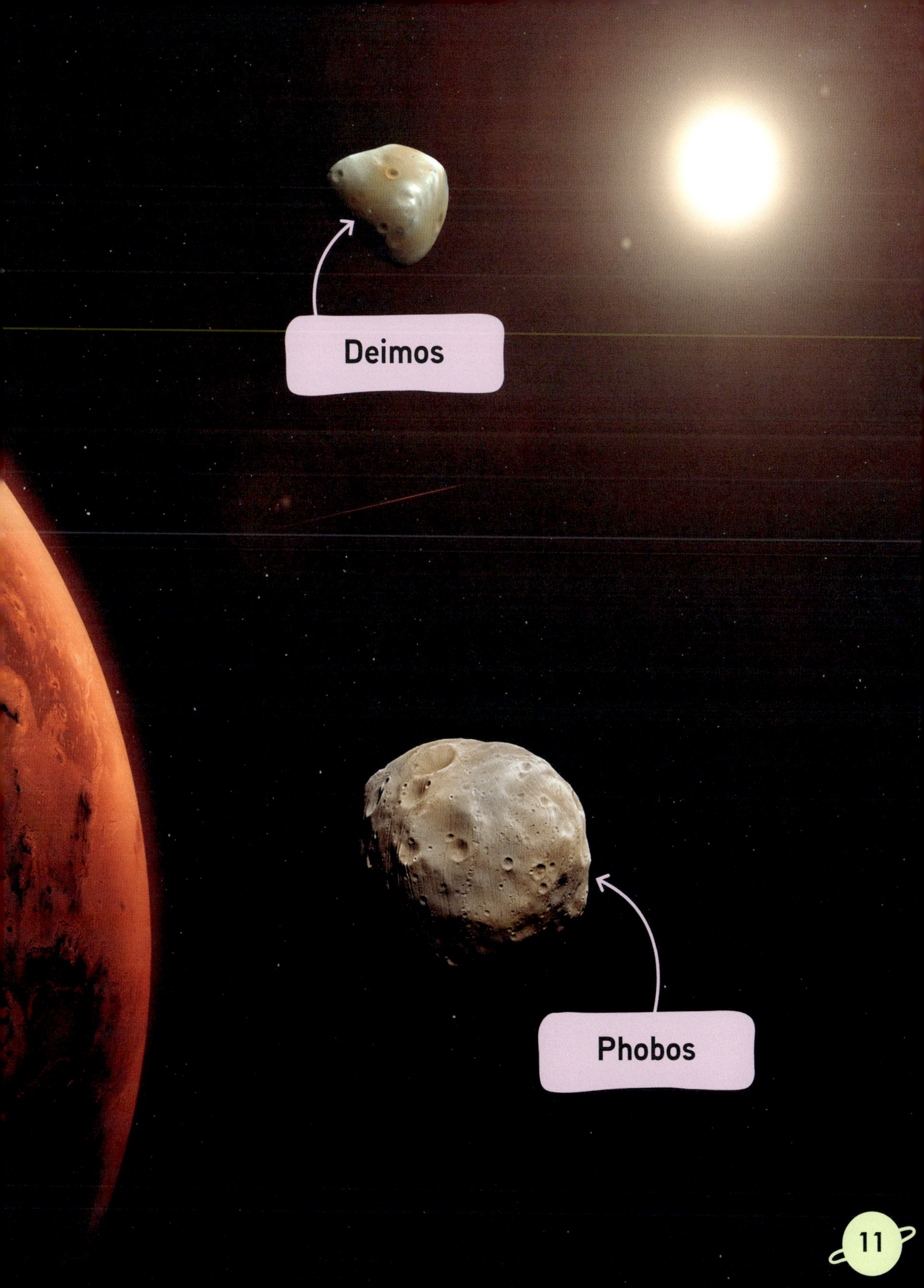
Deimos
Phobos

ON THE SURFACE

There are lots of volcanoes on Mars. The biggest, which is called Olympus Mons, is the tallest mountain in our whole solar system!

There are also lots of craters, created by rocks crashing into the surface.

There is also a huge **canyon**. It is 2,500 miles (4,023 kilometers) long and 7 miles (11 kilometers) deep – Mount Everest, the tallest mountain on Earth, could fit inside it!

Canyon

FACT FILE

Mars is the planet that scientists have studied the most in our solar system – apart from Earth of course!

Mars can be seen in the night's sky as a bright point of light that looks slightly red.

People in Ancient Rome believed that red was a symbol of war. They named the planet after their god of war, Mars.

Mars has something in common with Mercury, Venus, and Earth. The four planets closest to the Sun are all rocky planets!

LIVING ON MARS

Living on Mars presents scientists with some tricky problems to solve.

Mars's surface is too cold and has no air to breathe. Anyone traveling there would have to live inside a human-made shelter.

Water would be very hard to find too, and scientists would need to find a way of growing food there.

Not only that, it takes up to nine months to travel to Mars. It's 140 million miles (225 million kilometers) away from Earth!

WHAT CAN WE SEE?

If it's a clear night, it is possible to see Mars in the night sky even without a **telescope**.

Every two years, Mars travels slightly closer to Earth than normal. This is the best time to see it!

If you look through a telescope, you can see the ice at its poles and its dark patches.

Ice on Mars

LANDING ON MARS

Mars's thin atmosphere makes it difficult to slow down a spacecraft that is trying to land. But it is possible!

In July 1971, Viking 1 landed successfully. It sent back lots of data and photographs, and was the first mission to test the soil on Mars.

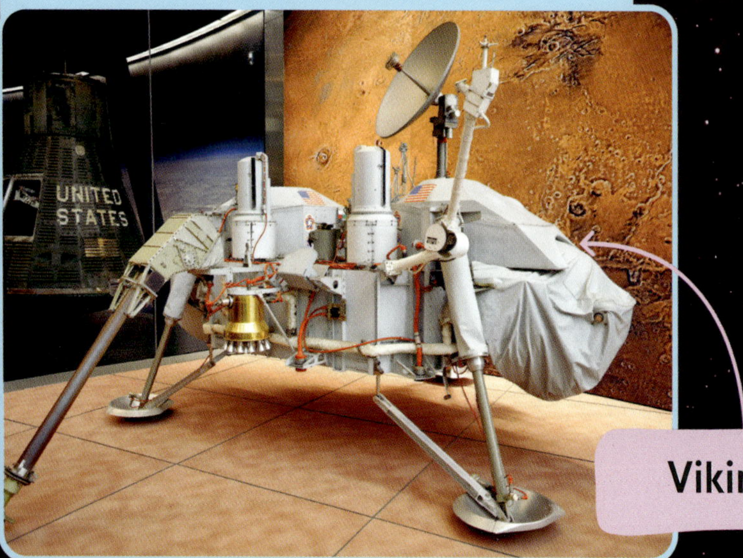

Viking 1

In 1997, the Mars Pathfinder spacecraft took a **robot** vehicle to Mars. It tested rocks to help scientists learn more about the planet!

WHAT'S NEXT?

NASA's Perseverance Rover and Ingenuity helicopter landed safely on Mars in 2021!

Ingenuity was the first human-made **drone** to fly on another planet. It completed 72 flights before being damaged by a rough landing. It can't fly anymore!

Ingenuity

Perseverance is on a mission to find out if there was once life on Mars by collecting rock samples. Getting these samples back to Earth will require other missions currently being planned by different **space agencies**.

GLOSSARY

Asteroid belt – an area between Mars and Jupiter where lots of space rocks can be found.

Asteroids – small space rocks that orbit the Sun.

Atmosphere – the gases that surround a planet or star.

Canyon – a long and narrow valley with steep sides.

Carbon dioxide – an invisible gas in the air.

Craters – large holes that have been created by something hitting the ground.

Drone – a small, flying robot.

Earth days – the amount of time that a day lasts for on Earth (24 hours).

Moons – large, natural objects that orbit a planet.

Mountains – rocky landforms that rise high above their surroundings.

NASA – the National Aeronautics and Space Administration is an agency that deals with space exploration.

Orbit – the path taken by one object circling around another object in space.

Poles – the points furthest north and south on a planet.

Robot – a machine controlled by a computer that can do tasks on their own without a human.

Solar system – the Sun and everything that moves around it.

Space agencies – organizations that design and launch missions to explore space.

Telescope – instruments that make faraway objects appear bigger.

Picture credits:
(t=top; b=bottom; m=middle; l=left; r=right):

NASA: images-assets.nasa.gov/image/PIA16610/PIA16610~orig.jpg 10bl; images-assets.nasa.gov/image/PIA02895/PIA02895~~orig.jpg 12bl. Shutterstock: Alones 14-15bg; Artmim 16-17bg; Artsiom P 6-7bg, 12-13bg, 22bl, 24bg; AstroStar 18-19bg; Buradaki 7tr, 10-11bg, 15tr; Fordelse stock 9tl; Fukume 22-23bg; gidenilson 4-5bg; HAKAN AKIRMAK VISUALS 18bl; Luca Fabbri 14bl; Max-min stock 20ml; NASA Images 1bg; Paopano 17tr; Sima zel 2-3bg; Studio Peace 16bl; Vadim Sadovski 20-21bg; Wlad74 8-9bg.

Every effort has been made to trace the copyright holders, and we apologize in advance for any unintentional omissions. We would be pleased to insert the appropriate acknowledgments in any subsequent edition of this publication.